AF362976

Imagined Dreams & Forgotten Futures

Priyanka Kumar

BookLeaf Publishing

India | USA | UK

Imagined Dreams & Forgotten Futures ©
2024 Priyanka Kumar

All rights reserved.

No part of this publication may be
reproduced, stored in a retrieval system, or
transmitted, in any form or by any means,
electronic, mechanical, photocopying,
recording or otherwise, without the prior
written permission of the presenters.

Priyanka Kumar asserts the moral right to
be identified as the author of this work.

Presentation by *BookLeaf Publishing*

Web: www.bookleafpub.com

E-mail: info@bookleafpub.com

ISBN: 9789363304574

First edition 2024

PREFACE

It is a true privilege to love another unconditionally.

Love gives rise to many things: joy, pain, loss, anger, arrogance, grief, delusion, illusion, and that is only scratching the surface. To truly love someone is to learn another person—to see them as they are. It's to help them at their worst, to celebrate them at their best, to push them up as they reach for their stars, and comfort them if they fail a test. To truly love someone is to feel the entire rainbow of consequences of that love and to know that every experience—without qualification—borne of that love is worth having.

It is true that sometimes love also leaves you disappointed, or in many unfortunate cases, heartbroken. But the ever-resilient heart will always pick up the pieces and continue shining light, provided one's pesky ego doesn't get in the way.

The reality is that love is everything and nothing.

In all my life—everything I have ever known—nothing has been as worthy a motivator. Love makes the world go round. It gives us the strength to wake up with the sun, go through mundane routines, and deal with unexpected spontaneous combustions in our everyday lives. Love in all its forms—familial, parental, platonic, romantic, sensual, requited or unrequited—is what paints the world in rich colours.

This poetry anthology is the culmination of many relationships, many experiences, and is wholly a labour of love, in every sense of those words. I owe its existence to everybody I have ever had the privilege of loving in my lifetime.

*For everyone I have ever loved, and
everyone who has ever loved me.*

absent frangipani

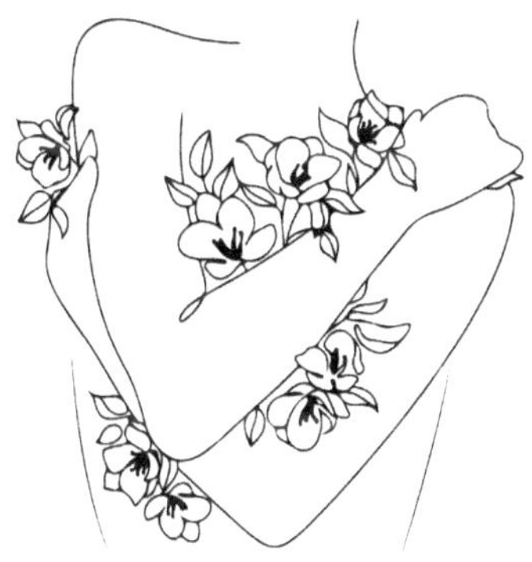

Your kind, brown eyes crinkled
as you smiled,
and the look on your face showed me
how well you knew me.

Your smile, bright, beautiful and gentle,
haunts me in the middle of the night
in my knowledge that I only ever
see it in pictures anymore.

Dreams are harder than reality
when you continue on
unfettered in one, but not the other.
And I have spent so many hours
trying to work out when this
pain will end—
only to realise there is no end.
No other way to be anymore
except in the truth of your loss.

My heart aches for the lost time,
and I sigh as the ground falls out
from underneath me.
Free falling through that vacuum,
through that lost space, is still
easier than this.
The missed heartbeats.

The last kiss on your forehead
as you lay on the ground,
your skin, cold and flesh, swollen.
You looked not like yourself,
but the painful outcome
of what you were forced to become.

As each tear falls
and splashes on my reality,
and I stand under the umbrella
of a fate and destiny
that I choose to believe in—

I picture your gentle smile,
and your warm brown eyes,
memorise the feel of your arms,
as you hold my heart in yours.
I walk through the gateway to
where I see you standing.
And I know we'll be with
each other again, one day.
In this crazy universe
you and I call Home.

soulmates past

I miss how we giggled like school girls,
laughing as we naively looked
to a future we imagined to be real.
We talked about how
we'd raise our kids,
we called ourselves *soulmates*
and to hell with the world.

Light shined from your eyes as you
smiled at me,
the tips of your teeth peeking out from the
innocence in your heart.
Fingers entwined in promises long broken
of trust, friendship, and love;
days long past, nights stretched into years.

Re-born now in different lifetimes,
we go through the motions.
We smile. We hug.
I miss you—I know.

Always only for yourself,
forgone the bond that we hopelessly clung
to
as our seventeen-year-old selves
look on helplessly.
We discard what once was for what is.

And as all those dreams and smiles,
those tears and fights
are engulfed in a sea of unshed
frustration of what we have become.

What we were lies crumpled
and tossed carelessly on the floor.
I know in my heart,
there is no us anymore.

problem child

Oh, problem child!
This heart of mine
lies cut open and bleeding
one more time.
Did you know?
In those days foretold
one day you'd become
a paper-thin ghost
haunting the hallways
of your imagined dreams and
forgotten futures;
reciting prayers,
psalms and hymns—anything,
to get you through yet another
awakening.

Oh, problem child,
go once more for the crowd,
who watch for every misstep,
squeezing droplets through
the drought of your dwindling fire.
The jackals and hyenas
who cackle behind presumed concern
and facetious responses
to your so-called problems.

Oh, problem child.
What must you know of the world?

Fallacious arguments in a fragile tapestry of
relationships dreamed up in your mind;
unnecessary expectation.
Skies crack open in thunder and lightning,
swathed in the tears of angered gods and
distraught goddesses
who sob at the sight of your surviving.

Oh, little problem child!
This heart of mine lies open and bleeding.
This time, unaffected by all your scheming,
forevermore to be hidden
in its imperfect beating.

striped childhood giggle

A soft hum under your breath.
The light wood against which you rest,
cushioned by cotton—striped with light
pinks and greens—
flailing arms and squeaked chirps.

Scrunched nose burrowing
into your lap as you worked.
My small head shifting and pressing down
to find the most comfortable spot.
Contorting and twisting until
every part of me fully fit into you.
Your annoyance; huffing,
because you had important things to do
and I was simply uncaring.

You still let me.

Pushing my head into your busy hand,
demanding,
your   fingers   seemingly   unthinking,
complying,
running through my hair that was not as
long as yours,
but was getting there.

One day.

From my lips, uncertain sounds
that in a different lifetime held a melody.
Your fingers are colder than they've ever
been.
Your eyes open, but unseeing.

Or are they?
I don't know anymore.

Your body lying on white
and grey stripes.
You on thin white I want to replace
with pink and green.
I clutch your freezing palms and
rub gently—
Just a little bit of warmth;
Barely enough.
Never enough.
And I pretend I've gone back
in time to sixteen.

My palm traces the rough texture
of the top of your head.
Short.
No longer growing.
Grey.

I fall back on your side.
Sharp pinch and a scowl.
I'm not as small as I once was.
        That hurts! Get up!
I grin.
        Nope!
Another giggle, as if I haven't grown at all.
And maybe around you, I haven't.
Maybe around you is when I'm allowed.
The only permission I would seek
and accept to simply be.

Soft melancholic love.
Familiar notes.
Familiar voice.
I glance over at the TV.
        This song again?
A look.
Your hand gently moves (un)happily up
and down my arm,
I throw it across your middle.

Careful, methodical—desperate—
calmness characterises my movements
more so than anything else does, I think.

Or perhaps it's that I can't see past it to any
other possibility.

Anything for you to be okay.
Anything so you will be okay.

Low and off-key.
Air from my lungs fills in the memory.
This again?
            And again.
                        And again.
                                    And again.

White coats check in periodically.
            How is she?

Dark wooden tables, blinking phones.
Late nights early enough to be mornings.
Wandering eyes to the last time we took a
picture together.

They say before we incarnate,
we choose our parents.
            Did I choose you?
They say before we are born,
we choose our life.
            Did you choose this?
Phantom soft skin beneath my palms.
            I think about death a lot.
Textured black hair underneath my fingers.
            *Specifically, I wonder what
consciousness feels like after death.*

Nails poking into sides.
        I think about how life experiences itself
in a form that is not physical.
Angry shouts at boundaries pushed too far.
        I think about how physicality is defined
in mainstream 'modern' rhetoric.
Inconvenient truths.
        I wonder about the energy of life after
death.
Even more inconvenient realities.
        And I think about those who are
untouched by all this.

        What are you singing?
But it's seeped into my bones.
        Nothing.

bittersweet misery

No one in this world
has the power over me that you do.
Yet no one but me
has seen as clearly through you.
The times we fight
land lightning strikes,
gashes through my heart.
With each spoken word,
they drive us apart.

No one in this world
holds you like I do.
You say you know me better
than I know myself,
and perhaps it's true, perhaps it's true.
Still the unspoken frustration
at yet another accusation
of once again being the reason
for life's unbearable treason—

What else could I possibly do?

The kingdom falls into mighty disrepair
          *Oh faithless traveller! Why weren't you
there?*
The sky breaks open in crashes of thunder
          *That catastrophic brunt was yours to
shoulder!*
A tree falls in the forest miles away—did it
even happen?
          *Oh ye blind to truth, your vision is
sorely lacking.*
The songbird forgets its birthright, its
melody
          *How could you not have predicted this
malady?*

Time and again,
it boils down to this.
Raised voices brushing against
the ceiling of a relationship
carefully rebuilt.
And I see my part in this play.
How I've caused the situation.
But what about you?
What about your station?
We change and we change
yet walk the same paths again.
An endless loop of scenery
so familiar
we constantly drift away
as we grow near.

And still I yearn
for this bittersweet misery.
For it's better than nothing at all—
for I live in the hope that one
day you will heal.

there never was another woman like you

There never was a woman like you.
Sharp tongue and sharper wit.
There never will be another
woman like you,
Beauty and grace unparalleled—
one must admit.

There never was a woman like you.
Splashing skies with wild abandon,
chasing dreams with an unapologetic air
streaked by wartime canons.

There never was a woman like you.
Fire inside that would burn alive
those who dared to question its existence.
Glowing brighter in front of
fools who test its resilience.

And when in my dreams
I see you laughing and smiling,
playing and fighting,
living your life—
stolen in a moment too quick.
I think to myself, I was right.

No.

No, there never was another woman like
you.

more

Reality checks in conversations with you
echoing my heart's aching truth.
In all this fear of what's to come—
how do I promise to go beyond?

Does arrogance cloud my ability to see
what lays itself out quite plainly before me?
How many ways would this life
be improved
if I chose to focus on me, not *you*?

Infallibly easy to point fingers
harder to see oneself in the mirror.
Joy solely dependent on my own action,
yet I cannot stop the dissatisfaction.

Of what I can't control, and that constant
contradiction.

Events out of my hands, still set in motion,
with a lasting impact that finds me frozen;
and that fleeting cherished quiet, stolen.

Looking in the mirror
Wide-eyed and unsure
How do I move forward?
How can I be *more*?

trauma dumping

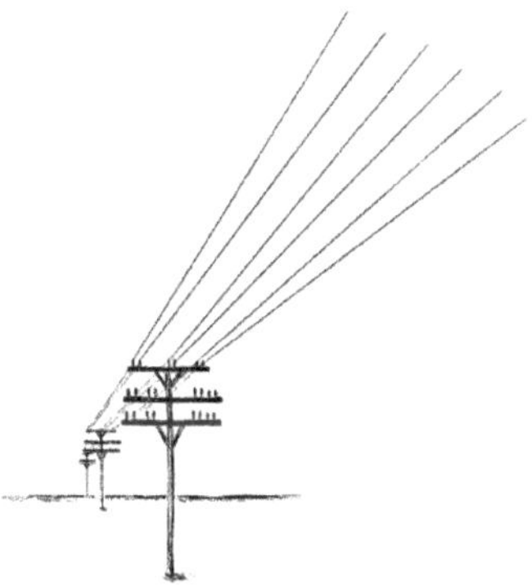

Coming back to your streets,
walking pathways previously
skipped over in the dark of midnight
under the light of the moon.

Oh, how you've changed!
Since the afternoons of my childhood,
filled with innocent laughter bouncing off
grey school walls and brick passageways.

Promises taken under duress,
broken of free will, to never return
churn within my stomach,
uncomfortably reminding me—
All is still not right.

But the stones I left unturned
crunch beneath my feet, with every step—
light or heavy,

in a never-ending cycle of emotion.

And still, I think I will,
I always will,
come running back to you.
Living wildly under the
orange-pink sunrise
of a forgotten childhood.

colourful patchwork

Breathing in your fragrance—
wafting through the grainy fog
and smoggy haze
of a dream that was born millennia too late,
in the hearts of those who would
only see this break.

A rich tapestry of lives so artfully
woven between
a turgid history of blood and swords;
by those who wielded their pens skilfully—
volumes hide their blatant discord.

But you, oh you, live deeper than the
wrongs of others.
You, oh you, birth greatness in travesty; the
ultimate mother.
From you, oh you, rise glory and abundance
resplendent.
Into you, oh you, we surrender our
intention, our beings ascendant.

Your magic, an open secret,
flows through lush greenery.
Your essence apparent only to
those who know it,
creates inimitable scenery.

Roaring rivers and trembling mountains.
Time-borne witness to cycles of creation
and destruction.
We see as you grow, wept as you fell,
listened as you shared
a lonely history only few know well.

And still, mother of mothers,
your infinite blessings bathe those
who learn.
For in your unconditional grace
we re-emerge with a raging fire to burn.

karmic debt

In the quiet of the world
crashing clouds break open
the great dark sky.
Those murky chambers Her fury belies.

Shifting and moving
as the earth is cleansed once more.
From the dearth of our hands
erupt ruptured promises once sworn.

She welcomes a new age.
A refuge for what has been broken.
She wails down upon us
fierce longing and commitment.

Fill in the cracks of hallowed ground
and feel out the future of Her cause.
To set right events in motion
and remind us of what once was.

And what will be again,
for what we are is nothing in
sight of who She is.
She wants neither cheap retribution,
nor capricious guilt.

Our arrogance has reached its boiling point,
with feeble structures forced

into Her womb.
In decisive wrath they come apart,
with certain folly, we build our tomb.

In the power of Her arms,
in the strength of Her vulnerability,
Her open chasm a deceptive calm,
Her self torn open for healing.

Her tears pour—the beating rain.
Her cleansing breath—the howling gales.
Her unwavering resolve—the rhythm
of our hearts.
Her gentle mercy—the wind in our sails.

She blows through these bodies
we fiercely attach ourselves to,
forgetting this life is impermanent,
forgetting all lies in Her Truth.

Her Divine context
our hubris refuses to see.
And only in it, my friend,
can we once again be free.

growing pains

I fell in love with so much about you.
I pictured bright sunny days,
long sleepless nights, curled up
in your arms.
My lips against yours, moving
with an intimacy I have
only ever imagined.

How wicked to paint my night
sky—counterfeit paradise,
only to shred it better than supplies
in an ageing government office,
ready to shut down
not a day too soon.

You ripped me to pieces
and blamed me for the fall.
Your words twisted in my mind,
told me I was wrong.
Every sound pierced my heart,
unflinching and cruel.

My self bent and buckled,
I couldn't explain it.
My heart was broken,
I didn't know it.
What you stole—
you did so well,
I didn't even know.

But as the sun rises over the horizon,
and light touches all
that was once enveloped in your darkness,
the weight of the future swirls in my palm
with heavy, groaning sighs.
But still I see the path ahead—
and for once I see it without your lies.

dynasty

The consequences of the sins
are rarely borne by the sinners.
In this universal truth and
this pantomime of justice,
only the best players are
crowned winners.

Memories fade away through time
with loved ones easily replaced.
If transience were a crime—
who would be the first to be
carted away into prisons forgone?
With cuffs slapped on wrists and
forced remembrance of vows long gone.

Paper planes crumple mid-air,
wings crash into windows
that once held bells and whistles
keeping lofty words, deduced
intentions afloat, and it's rare.

It's rare in this world of invoked pledges
and contractual connections,
that the transaction of our love
has become more than its fate.
Though it's unfortunate, really,
that it all happened in the wrong direction.

untold love

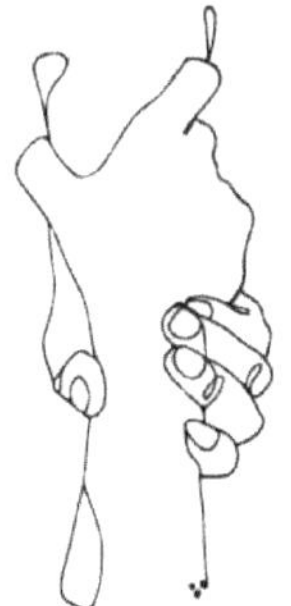

How I've watched you grow!
A cheeky pitter-patter of
footsteps that would sow
the seeds of a story yet to be told.

How I've learned that you see
the world in rich colours,
but hide them away tightly wrapped
and bursting at the seams.

How I've understood that you cry
when life pierces you so deeply,
even your strong, stubborn will
is powerless against its might.

How I've listened as you shared
unwitting truths you wouldn't
otherwise dare,
behind frustratingly polished words
and hopelessly transparent glares.

How I've felt as you moved
mountains for those you view
in the light of your heart.
It shines so true.

How I've known as you loved
those who earned it and those who don't,
without condition or care.
Staying true to your legacy—
the perfect heir.

convenience crush

Teenage dreams and wanton recklessness.
A gentle nudge and push
towards something special
only because you found the
extra in the ordinary.

Secret conversations for hours that turn into
days that turn into months that
turn into years—
all in your mind. With someone who
doesn't quite see all the ways
in which you're contrary.

Whispered moments all in between
imagined landscapes and realities unseen.
Wrapped up in a fragmented embrace
so tight it's bursting at the seams.

It's the magic in the everyday.
The possibility never otherwise considered
lest it play out into a future so happy—
perhaps it's better we let it all stay buried.

love letter to a friend

My dearest love,
I want you to know.
No matter what life may bring,
no matter what the future holds:
  Your heart has a fire that burns
  so bright
  Your eyes shine with the purest light
  You won't 'go gentle into that good
  night';

My firebrand of fate,
Did you ever consider?
Despite being so afraid
through all those tempestuous flickers:
  The worst of your fears will cower
  under the heat of your gaze
  The universe itself would tremble
  before your capacity to create;

My sunshine and moonlight,
     Your being is starlight
     with a passion that guides
     even the most desperate souls
     seeking salvation,
     in the ruins of thoughtlessness,
     lending hope to forlorn hearts
     with perfect translation;

My darling friend, my soulmate,
     I long for the day
     when the force that you are
     crafted to perfection by Mother
     Nature's divine grace,
     loves herself with a quiet knowing,
     lives in her own complete embrace.

girlhood

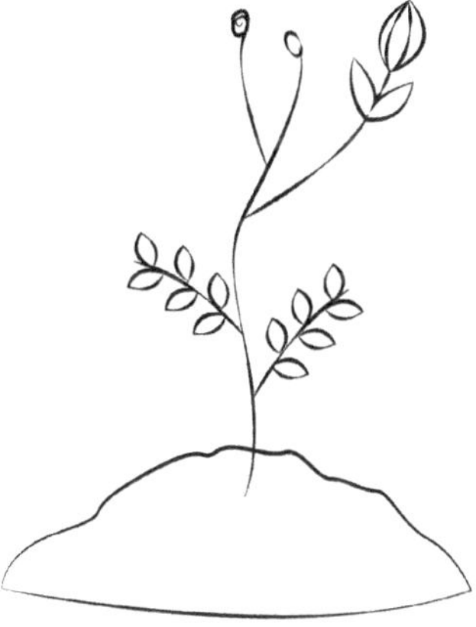

A shy giggle, a boisterous laugh.
Musical tittering that fills the air.
Long, stern, side-eyes and
unbecoming scoffs;
she who goes on without a care.

Always on the cusp
of what's past and what's new.
Circling vultures that swoop in
for the kill,
leaving with a begrudged view.

How dare you be happy in front of my face?
Silent (read: loud) shrugs,
complete with cherubic and
Cheshire smiles,
and (un)pretentious airs and grace.

Death glares and toxic personalities
wishing upon a star with
sanctimonious soliloquies.
Cheeky finger waves and false heroism,
diving deep into caverns of
fleeting emotion.

Only to come together when
all is said and done,
with fingers encircling wrists.
Tight hugs and stolen cheek kisses
slowly carry us over into mist.

dreamscapes in a clandestine midnight

You are the breeze from the lake
on a brisk winter morning,
the cool air brushing through my hair,
working it into knots I can't untangle
without hours of frustrating combing.
I'd go back every day if I could.

You are the smell of the white roses from the
JON's on Glenoaks Boulevard
that I've only been to twice in my life.
Nothing special, it holds me firmly
within its mundane embrace.
Because I only go there when I visit
people I love more than love itself.

You are the sound of that song that didn't
quite hit right the first time around,
but somehow growing up has made
all the difference,
dissonant heartbeats stutter in my chest.
Making words kiss the air,
making me hope for more than I
care to admit.

You are that smooth satin ribbon
that ripples along,

I can almost feel it on my skin.
The phantom caress of a lover's touch
that traces every insecurity I pretend
therapy has dissolved into nothing.

You are the pitter-patter of water splashing
when the rain pours down outside,
so heavy;
droplets hit the ground and
ricochet upwards
finding purchase on any exposed skin.
A wet blanket on my wavering belief.

You are the warmth of my thin sheet
layered with a blanket cocooning
me at night,
when the temperature is -1 Celsius out—
the ones I always kick off later so
the cool air of my apartment
will envelope my body enough that I
miss that warmth again.
A push and pull so natural, you no longer
even wake me up.

Asleep, frozen in a dreamscape of
nightmarish truths and utopian realities,
I see you. And I feel you.
And I—

Never to admit when the sun rises
on yet another morning of familiar

comfort zones and habitual denial that we
were ever real,
that this was ever something.

wishful thinking

You write some more
then close the door
in the wake of feelings
I've never felt before.

Write about us—
it's you and me
but want me to wait for eternity.

The wide, boxy smile that crosses your face
is more than I bargained for
but it's all I see
in the magic of this world
in the secrets of this space.

I want again for the moment
I can see your face.

I wish I were brave

I wish I were brave
enough to storm the wilds
of the highlands where your secrets hide.
Enough to sail the stormy seas
I see so clearly behind your smile.

The bright curiosity
of your light brown eyes.
The soft crinkles of your skin
I traced under the moonlight.

Your gentle calm—such contrast
to my chaotic night.
It cuts so cleanly through the fog
of my mind trapped in fight or flight.

But dearest heart—
How I wish you could see,
most of all,
I wish I were brave enough
to ask if you could love me.

paperweights on a broken
heart

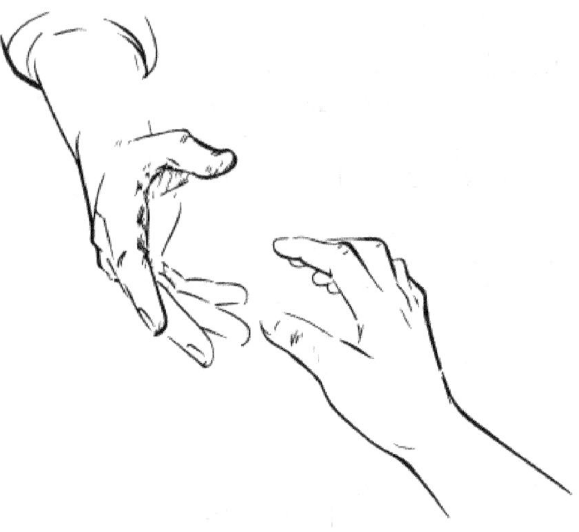

Zen gardens in white and beige.
Too-bright sunlight and hope in your heart.
Auto-rides in a misty haze,
all with the wish I would add myself
to the chart of your life,
take my rightful place as your wife.
In this world full of fakers and shakers,
we might have become
a supernova colliding,
resigned to the fate of
a black-hole collapsing
in on itself when pen is finally
put to paper.

Weary smile as you told me about her.
It's really hard losing your mother.
I know.
But were that enough to build
something together.
In my stock pile of closet utopias,
I lost that version of me,
the one I'd have to be to have you,
years ago to nostalgia.

Salacious greetings that sound indelicate
A wry chuckle at the reality
that we never got far enough
for you to be scandalised by me.
Maybe in a different life,
where my demons didn't have
butcher knives
sharpened in the same starlight
my heart lives in.
Maybe in a different life,
these broken hearts are mended,
held together and headed
for a future that is more than
the worst of someone else's sins.
Maybe in a different life
the threads of our fate intertwined,
finding us blissfully ignorant
of the alternate universe in which
the story of us died.

Maybe in a different life,
we survived.

nameless / placeless / timeless

When the soft white of the clouds
open out into the wide blue of the sky,
it is only then I can breathe in the truth of
my self and my home.

Like a bird finding her wings in
the great, wide beyond,
my heart is full when it belongs to no one.

Pulled in either-or-every direction,
constant inconstancy and motion.
What is this world in which
those who bridge,
those who connect,
don't fit in?

Tongues wag when mine speaks—
Where is the old you?
The familiar you?
I know as little as you do, my friend;
yet I am still *me*.

Skin, self, mind, and body,
different from those I live amongst.
The land of opportunity, the melting pot
of cultures!
You wouldn't know melting pot if it hit you in
the face.

And so, I make my home among the clouds.

The one place I am asked of nothing.
The one place I am asked for nothing.
The one place where those who bridge
are accepted.
The one place where those who bridge
just Be.

dreamless truth

Woken up from the deepest slumber,
a heart that bursts open
as flames run unencumbered.
But only to warm. Never burn.

Unbearable lightness of being,
stars that shine bright
with unexpected meaning.
Pure white in the deepest trenches
ever seen.

Closeted fears that don't translate
into a newfound level
beyond hope and faith.
The truest wish granted, not a
moment too late.

A knowledge so true—
the easiest choice to ever make in lieu
of mindless chatter,
opening into a sky so blue.

Oh, Joyful Heart!
How wonderful to finally meet you!

abundant landscapes

In a simple moment,
the truth of its existence
is apparent.
I have spent hours of my life
searching for signs,
finding words that encapsulate
that fleeting feeling—

The one that started wars
and ended revolutions.
The one that opened universes,
built towering castles in a land-locked sky.
In lands once barren,
forest sprouted where mud ran dry
and love rung out
across a long, streaked night.

Living in doubt so long,
not once did the thought occur
to contemplate its existence
in the silence of my own.
Now here I rest,
my heart wide open at the expanse,
the infinite.

spoken hearth

The words have to feel right.
They have to sit perfectly in my mouth,
leaving just the right sensation.
It's not about the sound, you see,
or rather, not *only* about the sound.

Loquacious — talkative
Slippery like water gushing underneath
me as I squeeze down one of those
water slides you hated.
Or better yet, an eel.
Like it'll slip out of my mouth
and be gone before my tongue has
a chance to wrap around it completely.
Loquacious when I left home,
excited enough that my heart danced out
the rhythm of a future I had not yet lived,
with a past I didn't know
I would hunger for
with every fibre of my being
when it was gone.

Leaving you behind with the knowledge
that eighteen years were over,
and I'd slipped through
your fingers like silk
you'd spun with your heart
that you still couldn't quite get a grip on.

       *Sanctimonious — hypocritically pious
or devout*
Bright highlights that are not quite there.
They change on me constantly.
If I open my eyes and unclench my hands,
will they disappear into the nothingness
they came from?
Sanctimonious the feeling of
transient dreams.
I remember when you questioned
how I could claim to love writing,
how I could profess to want to be
good at it,
when I didn't have a
half-decent vocabulary.
It's been years since the sharp knife
of your frown
and weight of that sentiment
rolled so easily off your tongue.
Years since you so easily had me question
what I thought I knew about myself.

       *Emphatic — very expressive; using
emphasis*

Forceful gusts of wind—they move.
Quickly.
Emphatic—a large gust of warm air.
Like when it's freezing outside.
I exhale shakily,
trying to warm up my too-cold extremities
that I inherited from you.
I wish I had been enough to make
one goddamned difference,
amongst the white fluorescent lights,
the soft beeping,
red and green lines that hold far too much
power.
The ones that spoke too many words
without making nearly enough sounds.
        And they feel like *nothing*.

        Ameliorate — to make better or more
tolerable
Golden.
Expansive.
Bright and all-pervasive.
This one is special.
It's the warmth that bloomed
in my chest at your broad smile
and quiet contentment.

        Ameliorate. It's such a beautiful word.
Spoken sound. Simple word. Tactile feeling.
        Ameliorate.
It feels like love. Feels like healing.

fairy ring of joy

Limpid pools of sunlight filtering through
the sands of time in motion,
clearing away the threat of a cold monsoon,
pulling tighter that elusive thread
of devotion.

Beauty in the silence of the beholder,
tired of begging for yet another shoulder
to cry on as her mind wakes up
to the sinking pirate ship of her truth—
even that which was wrongfully stolen
cannot be returned—
lost to the turbulent anger of
unconditional love left cruelly spurned.

Crisp air, crisper leaves
fall and settle beneath
soft spread blankets and
cartons of irreplaceable Suleimani tea.
Breathing life into tired lungs
suffocating in familiar treachery.

Yet in the quiet brew,
grey clouds chased away by warmth,
offer a new beginning in lieu
of mindless patterns
and undue censure.
Perhaps happiness is just
a simple pleasure.

Home is where the heart is

In the quiet chirping of the birds,
and the wide blue expanse of the sky,
my heart is connected to you
in a way I neither know, nor understand.

Solitude in your arms is my paradise.
Working in your love is my preservation.

Leaving you is heartache: acute
and painful pangs
that radiate out from my centre.
They flood my senses and cloud my eyes
with emotions and feelings, which
if felt all at once
would rip me apart.

But through this, we are connected.

My love strengthens in yours.

My heart expands in yours.

My mind stretches in yours.

And my being centres in yours.

different kind of love

In bits and pieces, I envision
a future in which he and I have
a shot at something *real*.
My fingers run through his hair,
lightly trace the contours of his face,
resting momentarily on that dimple
appearing as his grin widens into
a full-blown smile.

In those imagined states,
as he takes on the role of you—
I wonder who you are,
and who we'll be.

When the nights get cold and lonely,
I curl up, wrapping textured sheets closer
around my shivering form,
I wonder where we'll go,
and which stars we'll wish upon.
I wonder how many nights we'll have,
and what our home will be.
Will we fight about the television
being too loud,
whether you'll want frozen dinners
over what's made by me.

I wonder how many skies we'll see together,
and how many worlds we'll know together.

How many lives we'll live together,
and how many deaths we'll die together.

Picturing each step around the fire,
seven circles,
for seven lifetimes.
Each one promising a love
that transcends our everyday.
A love that mirrors only
Truth.

And when the day finally comes,
and it's time we return once more
to the unity from which we're born—
on that day, I won't wonder. I'll know.
You were my *it*.
And I finally found what
I'd been searching for.

honest prayer

They say when you meet your soulmate,
    your heart won't quicken,
    your breath won't shorten,
    you'll feel only peace.

I once walked away from a love,
    that burned with incendiary chemistry,
    that my heart yearned for in deep sleep,
    that was never mine to keep.

I've begged all the powers-that-be,
    for years and months and weeks,
    to find a love that I would one day know
    was perfect, just for me.

And then I met you.
    You who stole my lasting patience.
    You who pushed me to inexplicable
    irritation.
    You who became an unwelcome fixation.

Oh, how I met you,
    A man who walked with airs and graces,
    brimming with an attitude my friends
    hated;
    and a sweet silence that left me
    intoxicated.

When I met you,
    Life didn't turn on its head.
    I found no wind brushing through my
    hair, nor any emptiness in my bed.
    My eyes were not strangely coloured
    with rose-tinted glasses I'd grow to one
    day dread.

Because when I met you,
    I finally learned.
    It matters not who hurt you.
    It matters not which tables were turned.

My love! Because I met you,
    I now finally see,
    Whether or not we're meant for each
    other—
    What I seek has always been within me.

I guess, maybe

I always pictured you holding my children,
chortling with every full gurgle.
But I guess maybe, that's not in
the cards now.

I always wondered how sentimental
you'd get on our wedding days.
But I guess maybe,
I'll never get to see your face
as we make those vows.

I always imagined losing you would
be a wound that never healed.
But time has proven to me what I
could not see
for myself in the depths of my grief.

I miss the way you rolled your eyes.
But I see it every time I close mine—
hear your voice in my head on
Sunday mornings,
when I take too long to get out of bed.

I miss the way your head fell back
as you laughed.
But I hear its musical sound—
see it every time I giggle,
when I trip over myself as I dance.

I miss the way your face
contorted in a scowl
when I'd interrupt your busy
schedule for a cuddle.
But feel your hug anyway—
everyday—
when life bursts my blissful bubble.

If you'd asked me nine years ago,
if I'd ever see the light,
after it dimmed on the seventh of July,
I'd have scoffed and cried.

But I guess, maybe,
today it's genuinely okay.
Because even in your absence,
you've taught me how to thrive.

she

Your eyes light up when you see me,
and it's all I can do to keep
my heart safe in my chest,
lest I fall for you—again, and again,
and again.
Were I so lucky to feel that kind of love.

You smile and the world is okay.
We balance out
what lies rippled within me.
So seemingly effortlessly,
and I'm left breathless.

I worry.
I'm too intense; my emotions too much.
My words—what's spoken,
misheard and misread.
But I breathe, and you know.
I sigh, and you understand.

With you, I can leap in the knowledge
and faith of honesty, of acceptance;

I'm not too much.
I'm not too much!
And you—
You are my light.

I gesture at you and say,
She. She's my best friend.
And then I look at myself and smile,
because I must have done
something right.

self love

Golden ripples of sunbeams
that light your face in a soft glow.
Wind in your hair on the back of a scooter
as your heart soars.

Clouds gently opening up above
giving cover, modest showers.
All for that moment of peace,
of freedom—always when you need.

It's the moment that the first rain
kisses your face,
leaving you drenched in its infinite grace.
It's the moment the gentle breeze
soothes your scraped knees,
with temporary pain indelibly erased.

It's when the moon circles back around
in the darkest midnight,
illuminating the pitch black
with the brightest white light.

It's when the light shines down
on your deepest flaws.
But leaves them open,
accepts them with love.

ACKNOWLEDGEMENT

A big thank you to my family—particularly my late mother, my father, my brother, and my sister-in-law—and my friends (you know who you are) for being my number one supporters from day one.

A special thank you to Gabby and Divya for always being my first eyes on a project.

Stepping in the direction of one's dreams takes a village. I'm ever grateful for mine.

www.ingramcontent.com/pod-product-compliance
Lightning Source LLC
LaVergne TN
LVHW021213200726
843509LV00012B/1437